# *Where the Money Grows*

## and

# *Anatomy of the Bubble*

# WILEY INVESTMENT CLASSICS

# *Where the Money Grows*

and

## *Anatomy of the Bubble*

Garet Garrett

John Wiley & Sons, Inc.

This book is printed on acid-free paper. ∞

Foreword © 1998 by Christopher M. Byron.
Published by John Wiley & Sons, Inc.
*Where the Money Grows* was originally published in 1911
by Harper & Brothers. "Anatomy of the Bubble" was
originally published in *A Bubble That Broke the World*
in 1932 by Little, Brown, and Company.

*Library of Congress Cataloging in Publication Data:*
Garrett, Garet, 1878–1954.
 Where the money grows and anatomy of the bubble / Garet Garrett.
  p. cm.—(Wiley investment classics)
 Includes index.
  ISBN 0-471-23897-X (cloth : alk. paper).—ISBN 0-471-23898-8
 (paper : alk. paper)
 1. Wall Street. 2. Speculation. I. Title. II. Series.
 HG4572.G3 1997
 332.64′273—dc21                               97-19053

10 9 8 7 6 5 4 3 2 1

# Contents

# Foreword

For a writer, there are few things in life at once more hopeful and humbling than to encounter someone who has said it all before—as in, after Shakespeare, why try? Something of the same reaction awaits anyone who makes his living writing about the world of Wall Street and high finance, and happens upon the slim volume entitled *Where the Money Grows.*

Lurking within these 50 plus pages—barely a book at all by contemporary publishing standards—is to be found the whole pantheon of human personality as it is shaped (and often misshaped) by the hunting down and getting of money. There are the Mike Milkens of Wall Street, the John Gutfreunds and the Michael Steinharts, the Ivan Boeskys and the Joe Jetts. They're all there—the grand parade of

Wall Street money men as the 20th century draws to a close.

The thing is, *Where the Money Grows* was written not at this century's end, but at its beginning—at a time when stock quotes still traveled by ticker, and not every old-timer was yet prepared to concede the final triumph of the telephone and the adding machine as tools of modern commerce. Yet reading Garet Garrett's portraits of "The Manipulator" and the "Wolf," his picture of the "bank president" and the "hoodoo," one is reminded just how little anything has changed from that day to this. Remove the Quotrons and the Bloomberg terminals, get rid of the videoconferencing centers and the satellite uplinks, and the Wall Street of 1997 doesn't look all that different from the Wall Street of 1911, when Garrett wrote his book.

*Where the Money Grows* was Garrett's first book, written when he was 33 years old and working as a financial writer at the old *Evening Post*, his fourth such job in seven years. As resumes go, his was not one to inspire confidence in his staying power—at least at this stage of his career. Mostly what one comes away with is a picture of a nervous young man having trouble holding down a job: *New York Sun* (1903–1905), the *New York Times* (1906–1907), the *Wall Street Journal* (1907–1908), and the *Evening Post* (1909–1912). Then again, this was an age when financial writers—indeed journalists of all sorts—were still, in the literal sense of the word, "journeymen" with transportable skills, and employee loyalty was not among them.

Later in his life, Garrett's experiences congealed into a rather icy conservatism reminiscent of another newspaper curmudgeon, H. L. Mencken. Much of his thinking found expression in editorials he wrote for the *Saturday Evening Post* from 1940 to 1942, and later, the *American Mercury*. Along the way came four novels and maybe a dozen lesser writings, but of them all, the one that has stood the test of time remains his first, *Where the Money Grows*.

Oscar Wilde once remarked that journalism is the sweep of the second-hand on the clock of history, and that more often than not, journalists get the time wrong. And doubtless, it was out of a sense of the fundamental incompleteness of the journalistic experience—*journalitis interruptus*—that Garrett wound up taking the long step back from his daily work of financial writing to deliver what remains in many respects the definitive *tour d'horizon* of Wall Street and the creatures who inhabit it.

What one notices most of all in *Where the Money Grows*—notices from indeed the first sentence of the book—is the *maturity* of the writing. And sentence after sentence it continues, as if Garrett were giving vent to a dammed up river of expression that simply had been unable to escape into the world of second-day leads and the "Five 'W's" of deadline writing in the inverted pyramid format. Consider the following as a "thesis paragraph" for an extended essay—which is what *Where the Money Grows* really is—and you have a case study of a skilled literary stylist breaking free for the first time from the shackles of journalistic convention. What is Garrett's book about? It's about this:

> The easiest way into Wall Street is by the Hall of Delusions, through which many have entered who forgot to return. That door stands always wide open. No legend of warning affronts the eye. There ought to be one, and it should read: "No Safe Conduct Here."

One thinks in that moment, not simply of a "Caution, Do Not Enter" sign, but perhaps of Cerberus—the three-headed dog that stands guard at the gates of Hades—for beyond those snarling teeth lie the riches (and ruins) of the American El Dorado.

Begin with Garrett as he enters this Hall of Delusions by way of New Street, where today loiter the jacketed floor traders and runners of the New York Stock Exchange when they move into the street for a breath of fresh air. Writes Garrett of New Street, which was as much a loitering ground 80 years ago as it is today, "In New Street all men are equally under the delusion that the ticker is a source of wealth— that wealth is made and unmade by the going up and down of prices."

On Wall Street, life is democratic, in that the 10-share odd-lot trader can have insights as valuable as those of a 10,000-share a day block trader. The odd-lotter's only limitation is that of the amount of capital he has available to invest. Thus writes Garrett, on New Street, "[a] speculator who does his ten thousand shares a day on the Stock Exchange will suffer himself to be harangued by a little speculator with a ten-share mind, and may debate with him the fundamentals of finance. A broker who has just executed a five-hundred-thousand dollar commission will stop to ask a put-and-call man what he thinks of the market."

Only beyond the portals of the great investment banks of Wall Street does the veil of democracy fall away. Writes Garrett, describing, in a universally appreciated word picture, the intimidation any outsider is intended to feel upon entering such an establishment: "About a large private banking house in Wall Street there is an air of omniscience as if nothing unexpected could ever happen. Doors do not slam, men walk softly upon rugs, voices are never lifted in feverish excitement over profit and loss; no one is permitted even to call off prices from the tape. There is first a feeling of space, quite different from that sense of limited margins which pervades a broker's office. Ceilings in a banking house are higher than ceilings anywhere else."

Who among us has not been in such a place? Has not felt one's stature grow suddenly smaller as the door to the main vestibule swings silently open on its oiled hinges to reveal the oak paneling and wainscotting beyond, as the imperious greeter approaches in a somber suit to ask what business we may have in such an establishment as this. Yikes!

Contrast that picture with Garrett's portrait of the haunts of a Wall Street "Manipulator." Here one finds not intimidation but secrecy—the same secrecy that shrouded the likes of Martin Siegel and Ivan Boesky as they met in darkened corners to exchange suitcases of money for insider tips on pending takeovers. Writes Garrett of such places, "Of all the queer shops in the world, the queerest is that of the manipulator. There is only his name on the door (not always that) unsupported by any connecting legend. If the law required every person to display a sign over his business door it would puzzle the manipulator what to put on his. Information Utilized To The Highest Advantage . . . Dealer in Prices, Architect of Markets, Pool Manager, and Consulting Expert."

In the end, the portrait of Wall Street found in *Where the Money Grows* is a portrait of business itself. Is there not a "wolf" in every line of work—the fellow who forces the envelope on law and limitation, and is in an unuttered manner actually respected for his audacity . . . the cowboy who says, "I work best alone"? Says Garrett of such a man, "No great Wall Street personages can afford to be seen publicly with the wolf, or even to recognize him in the street, but more of them know him, and are known to him than you would easily believe."

Similarly, consider the book's final, and in some ways most poignant chapter of all, "Taking Trouble Home." Not so many years ago the Connecticut novelist Erica Jong observed—in a memorable image of what it means to be a post-modern man who commutes to New York—that the men get up each morning, scrape the hair from their faces, and go out hunting for money. In "Taking Trouble Home" we find Garrett's rendering about what happens when the hunter of Wall Street returns empty-handed: the understated fury at a wife whose pose of naivete masks outrage at the failure . . . a portrait of a marriage in the incipient stages of collapse.

So settle back, put your feet up, and delve into this universal landscape that a now-forgotten financial reporter stumbled upon nearly a century ago. You can traverse it in an hour, if even that, but the footprints you'll follow will be as fresh on the earth as if you'd taken the downtown express only this morning and followed the throng as it split and disappeared into a thousand doorways in search of life's dreams. As Garrett puts it, "Life's illusions are all of the same sheer stuff; variety is a trick of refraction."

—Christopher M. Byron
September 1997

# *Where the*
# *Money Grows*

# Before the Opening

IN WHAT more or less follows, the connecting thread is a purpose to show how familiar illusions refract upon the Wall Street lens, and how the Stock Exchange mind may be affected by the material in which it works. Except as they practise the trade of money with strange, three-edged tools, Wall Street folk are like other folk who happen to be anywhere else. The secret of understanding is to get their point of view.

The easiest way into Wall Street is by the Hall of Delusions, through which many have entered who forgot to return. That door stands always wide open. No legend of warning affronts the eye. There ought to be one, and it should read: "No Safe Conduct Here."

The easiest way out is at the end of the book. Between here and there are a Hoodoo, a Banker, a Wolf; descriptions of things and of people only as queer as true, hearsay of things which perplex the belief, and a conclusion which ought to appear of itself, to wit: That everywhere life's illusions are all of the same sheer stuff; variety is a trick of refraction.

G. G.

# 1

# *The Hall of Delusions*

WALL STREET, if spelled with a capital "S," is a district of vague delimitations. There is a Wall street proper which takes the little "s" and is only a street. It begins at Broadway, directly opposite Trinity Church, and runs to the Brooklyn Ferry, on the East River; but when one speaks of Wall Street broadly one means to include lower Broadway, Broad Street, Exchange Place, portions of William, Cedar, Pine, and Nassau Streets, and—the Hall of Delusions. That you would never find without specific directions. As you walk east down Wall Street from Trinity Church it is the first opening on the right. Stroll in. It is a thoroughfare by courtesy only, and belongs by usage to Wall Street people, but nobody will notice you unless you are a woman and pretty, at whom the idle telephone boys on the steps of the Stock Exchange "Ah!" and "Oh!"

It is the rear of the great New York Stock Exchange you see on your left; on your right are some of the tall buildings which make the sky line of New York. One cannot begin to see the tops of them. The Hall of Delusions is very narrow. You come to Exchange Place. On your right you have more of the tall buildings, but on your left only such of the despised old rookeries as have yet to be displaced by steel construction. In one of these was the Open Board of Brokers, forty years ago; the sign is there still. In others are the tailors, stationers, tobacconists, and small shopmen who cannot afford to pay higher rents elsewhere. There are also a few dark places below street level, where even yet one whose capital is reduced may wager a dollar on the going up and down of one share of stock, stop one's loss at ninety-five cents, and lunch on the remainder. The last tall structure on your right is the Standard Oil Building, and now you have come to the end and are at Beaver Street.

You have walked through New Street. That is the common name for the Hall of Delusions. Retracing your steps, you will notice that all buildings, new and old, stand with their rear elevations to New Street. From that circumstance it derives a sort of privacy and other advantages, and is the more suitably devoted to the uses of brokers, traders, put-and-call dealers, financial writers, failures, touts, tipsters, moribund speculators, men of mercurial fortunes, and all the other accidental human phenomena of a great market-place where wealth is continually changing hands.

In New Street all men are equally under the delusion that the ticker is a source of wealth—that wealth is made and unmade by the going up and down of prices. Therefore, men in New Street are democratic. A speculator who does his ten thousand shares a day on the Stock Exchange will suffer himself to be harangued by a little speculator with a ten-share mind, and may debate with him the fundamentals of finance. A broker who has just executed a five-hundred-thousand-dollar commission will stop to ask a put-and-call man what he thinks of the market. Only the Morgans, the Rockefellers, and the Harrimans of finance avoid New Street. Either they are not deluded or they are undemocratic. Though they may walk through any other thoroughfare of Wall Street unobserved, they would be recognized too familiarly here. Their names would echo behind them, and no telling what else.

Human litter is New Street's chief interest. Leaning against the Stock Exchange railing are the Closed Minds. They talk always of yesterday as a time when one could have made money, and perhaps did, but they talk to themselves. They appear as punctually at ten o'clock as any broker, and vanish at three, making their day of it. Their delusion is that Wall Street could not open or close without them. They are pensioned by their wives, who, to be rid of them, give them car-fare each morning. Some of the wives are believed to have had money before marriage, in other cases the men are said to have made money before their minds closed and settled it upon their wives, and in other cases it is suspected that the wives take in sewing.

One of the Closed Minds will tell you, stranger as you are, that for twenty years he was a big money maker and took home each day from ten dollars to one thousand until he had counted two hundred thousand dollars, which his wife put away; now she will not live with him. He borrows his living in fractional currency. Another of the Closed Minds begins always in the same way, thus: "When I was with Cammack—" Another knew Harriman when he had not a dollar to speak of, was more interested in horseflesh than finance, and smelled of the stable; he doubts if Harriman was the great man people think he was, but he was undoubtedly lucky. Another has a method to beat the market which you can see for yourself by his chart would have been infallible for twenty years.

There are others whose delusions still excite them. There is one who comes each morning to New Street to find only fifty dollars, with which he will make fifty thousand dollars in a year, and never come again. He will tell you it is harder to make fifty dollars than fifty thousand dollars. Then there is a man who makes ten thousand dollars a year without capital and cannot tell you how he does it. On an active day you might find him with a thousand dollars' worth of puts and calls suspended in the air, so to speak, or financed with nothing more than his word that when the buyer pays he will pay the seller. He keeps messengers running to and fro—messengers of forty-five, who go errands for a quarter each, but who once had control of the put-and-call business as the man who makes ten thousand dollars a year without capital now has. In New Street the money-getting faculty is so finely spun that it may break in the night, and one does not know it until one has ceased to make money any more.

If you have expected to find in New Street old bricks in loose mortar, mellowed masonry, and architectural romance you are disappointed, because its walls have been so often replaced with higher walls to get the full earning-power of real estate. Changes of that sort, however deplorable, are still powerless against magic. Nothing happens in Wall Street but it will instantly echo in this deep little cañon. Between ten and three o'clock ask a regular New Street man the price of any active stock and he will tell you to the eighth, though he may not have seen a ticker for an hour. If you think that wonderful, why, it is nothing. Ask him what any great banker or capitalist is doing in the stock market, and he will tell you that. The one thing is telepathy and the other imagination, if you like, but how account for the fact that you believe him?

# 2

# *Wall Street Habits*

ONE OF the many things taken for granted
about Wall Street folk is that they are volatile
beyond the average, and less subject to fixed habits
of thought and action than people anywhere else.
But one who knows them well, or has observed them
attentively, will be tempted to think differently. Just
in the way a man comes to Wall Street between
9 and 10 A.M. there is more habit than he may be
conscious of himself. For instance, a large number of
Wall Street folk commute by the Erie. Formerly
they had all to use the ferry, and so arrived by hundreds at the foot of Chambers Street. They crossed
West Street in a body always, and began then to
break up. Each man had his own way of reaching the
Wall Street district, by one of, possibly, five hundred

combinations in plane geometry. To be taken out of one's habitual way, through the insistence of a friend, were like getting started wrong out of bed. Thus, two men might halt at the corner of Chambers and West Streets, say "So long" or "Be good," and part, each for his own way to Wall Street, though their respective offices were two doors apart, or, perhaps, in the same building, and not meet again until the next morning.

When the Erie commuters began to be delivered on Manhattan Island by the McAdoo tubes there was a breaking up of old habits, and among all Erie commuters in finance and speculation there was no doing of anything right in the stock market until new ones were formed, so that a man could reach his Wall Street by habit again without the vexation of having to direct his feet.

Many thousands of people come to Wall Street by the Subway. There are four ways to emerge from the Wall Street Subway station, and once a man has habituated himself to one of them he never deviates. From the street level there may be ten ways to reach his office, and, by habit, he goes always the one way. If it is his habit to pass from the Subway station directly through the Manhattan Trust Building into New Street, and thence to his office somewhere in Broad Street, and to return in the afternoon by the same way, he may not see Trinity Church, at the head of Wall Street, once a year. If something happens to call him around to the head of Wall Street he is surprised to find that the First National Bank has added several stories to its building. A man whose office is in lower Broadway would be amazed to find several new office buildings around in William Street, and Pine Street might look very strange to a man whose office had been at the corner of Broad Street and Exchange Place for fifteen years. And when it is considered that the Wall Street district is only three blocks wide and six long, bounded on the north by Fulton Street, on the west by Broadway, on the south by Beaver Street, and on the east by William Street, men's habits must be fixed, indeed, that they may do business at one side of it for years without ever seeing the other side.

Two men accidentally meet for the first time in three years.

"Where have you been all this time?" one of them asks.

"Well," says the other, "we moved over into Pine Street, you know, and somehow I can't get around to see you any more."

Pine Street is only the next street over, but it may seem as far from a man's habitual way of going and coming as a day's journey. The second man says:

"That's so; I had forgotten. I seldom get around that way."

On some quotation boards stocks are displayed in alphabetical order, on others in geographical groups, as "Grangers," "Pacifics," "Coalers," etc.; on some boards the stocks run down and on others across. Traders become accustomed to a certain arrangement, and are bewildered before a strange quotation board. That is a matter of habit. Some houses do not have quotation boards; the clients watch the market on the tape. A man who has become accustomed to watch quotations on a board complains that he cannot "see" the market on the tape, or *vice versa*, which is all a matter of habit. Tape-gazing becomes a habit—one of the most painful to observe. No matter how dull the market may be, a man will watch the tape. Impatiently he will pace the floor, berate the market for being so inactive, declare there is nothing to see, and then return to the tape to gaze at it steadily for another half-hour. This habit becomes at length so strong that a man will gaze at the tape after the market has closed. He is probably thinking; the act of thinking has become associated with the act of regarding the tape, and he is unconscious of staring for fifteen minutes at the ticker operator's last word, "Good-night."

There is a nervous habit peculiar to brokers on the floor. It is very odd. Every broker or trader on the floor carries in his hand or in his pocket a bunch of that coarse paper, cut 2½ × 3½ inches, on which all memoranda of purchases, sales, and quotations are roughly made. This paper is provided by the Stock Exchange in unlimited quantities. When a man on the floor is not otherwise employed with his hands he takes two or three sheets of this paper, folds them once, and tears them in two; evens them, and folds them, and tears them again, and then again, until he has a handful of the tiny pieces, which he either blows off his palm or flips into the air. Everybody does it, and does it continually, and at the end of a day on the Stock Exchange the floor is covered with those bits of paper.

One of the first things a man asks when he arrives in Wall Street, whether he says "Good-morning" or not, is, "What's London?" He refers to the London quotations for American stocks. They are either higher, lower, or unchanged, and he never gives it another thought. This is a matter of habit. It has been years since the London quotations for American stocks have had really any significance. Long ago, when the London market in American securities was more important than our own, it mattered whether London was up or down, but London quotations represent nowadays only the petty trading of an arbitrage crowd.

Whether habits of thought are any less rigid than habits of action among Wall Street folk is open to question. There would be much to say in the negative. It might be said that a large majority of those who come daily to Wall Street have but two habits of thought. One is the habit of thinking that the stock market will rise because the "big interests" have all the stocks and will advance prices in order to unload on the public, and the other is the habit of thinking that the market will go down because the "big interests" have succeeded.

# 3

# *The Hoodoo*

IN NEW STREET, which is the hallway of Wall Street, one may observe the hoodoo. From ten to three o'clock he leans against the area railings and acquires the brand of his misfortune, which is a horizontal, threadbare line across his coat at the small of the back. There is about him an air of departed prosperity which is unmistakable. What manner of existence he has from 3 P.M. to 10 A.M. is no other man's concern. Nearly everybody knows him. He was once a member of the New York Stock Exchange, or the son of one, or what's-his-name that was Gould's broker twenty years ago. He is most knowing of speech and would easily fool you if you were not warned. All the past he understands, and the why of everything, but for the present and future he is a source of fatal ideas and a borrower of money.

There is an indestructible fiction that Wall Street people are superstitious. Ask any Wall Street man if this is true and he will deny it lightly. Ask him if he believes in hoodoos and he will become petulant. But take him off his guard and ask him if he ever knew a hoodoo. He has—many a one. He can tell you more strange things about the individual hoodoo than were ever imagined. He recalls two whose presence in his office threatened to deprive him of all his other clients. He tried to break the spell for at least one of them. He bought 100 shares of Sugar for one, and sold 100 shares of Sugar for the other, at the same time and at the same price, on his own credit, in order that one of them should be bound to make a profit. Both of them lost. How? Well, it would be a long story. He recalls a certain broker, a fine fellow, who ran the gamut of misfortune, and had at last to sell even his furniture. His chairs matched the chairs of another broker, who bought them for that reason. He cared nothing for a hoodoo. But he was very sorry afterward. "No, indeed," says the broker, "there is no doubt that some people are just hoodooed."

Then ask him why a hoodoo is. How does he account for it? He does not account for it, exactly, but if it is past three o'clock and not later than four, and the day has been not unprofitable, he may tell you something like this: Somewhere in Wall Street is the voodoo tree. Botanists know nothing about it; they know only what they see, and the voodoo tree is invisible. Many unreasonable superstitions have fastened upon it, as, for one, the superstition that it feeds upon eighths and is the monster that gets the eighth which you, as the broker's client, so often think you have lost, which he, the broker, never finds, and is forever missing.

The evil power of the voodoo tree lies in its shadows, which, falling upon the unwary one, deprive him of that which may be loosely defined as the money-making gift. There are degrees of blight. One who has been touched but lightly may lose only half the gift, or two-thirds of it, so that instead of becoming a total failure he is simply much less successful than before. One upon whom the shadow has fallen full and dark is thereafter and forever without the gift. Offerings of propitiation are impossible, for, as you have been told, the voodoo tree is invisible. No man knows until afterward that he has been in its shadow.

There is the typical case of a man, now an obscure broker at fifty, who came to Wall Street when he was quite young to make a fortune. He had very little capital, but capital is nothing. He had the money-making gift. In three years, novice that he was, he won his fortune. He bought a place in Florida, another in Maine, and took a wife, with whom he set out for five years of travel. In his first year abroad news reached him that the house with which he had invested his capital for income had come upon difficulties. He returned to find that half his fortune was gone. Annoyed, but nothing more, he started where he had stopped. He could not do with less than his first fortune, because he had planned his life on a certain income. But, alas! unknowingly, he stood in the shadow of the voodoo tree. Whereas formerly everything that he did turned out so well, now nothing did he touch but to make a loss. After several months he desisted from speculation to think. He could not account for it. He tried again. Three times he tried and three times in vain, and then a bitter choice he had to make. He had enough capital to insure a livelihood if he were content to settle down and work for the remainder of his life as a broker of small means. Being married, he chose wisely, and he is a broker still.

It may be even worse. One who has tarried long in the shadow of the voodoo tree is not only deprived of the money-making gift for himself, but carries misfortune to others. That man becomes the hoodoo. He is a pathetic fact. Such a one was a cotton expert who, highly recommended, applied for a place with a Stock Exchange house that had bought a Cotton Exchange membership and wanted a man to open a new field of speculation to its clients. The applicant was in every way desirable, save for the fact that three houses with which he had been connected had failed, though not one for a dishonorable reason. He was rejected as a hoodoo. Shortly afterward he made a connection with another house to fill a similar want and proved a very valuable man in his sphere, but within a year the fourth house failed.

*The Hoodoo*

The hoodoo is often a man who everybody likes, speaks well of, and recommends to every one else, with the one reservation—he is a man who unaccountably has not succeeded. There is nothing whatever against him else; he is honest and shrewd, and everything but successful. Alas, the fact of his being unsuccessful damns him with all his qualities. Wall Street people may or may not be superstitious, but they think it pays to associate with success and avoid failure in its personal embodiment. The hoodoo, once he becomes known as such, must attach himself to the new-comers—those who do not know, have not been warned, or who are so new and confident as not to care. Each connection he makes will be a little less desirable, until he has reached the stage at which he is ashamed of his associations, having made them in the demi-monde of finance because he could make them nowhere else. Even they fail him at last, and then you meet him in New Street.

# 4

# *A Bank President*

O N   F I N E  mornings the president of a large Wall
Street bank may dismiss his automobile at
Seventy-second Street and Broadway, descend into
the Subway, tender his nickel, and submit physically
to the platform guard. He is pushed aboard a train
through the side door, and hangs by a strap like anybody else. When he emerges from the Wall Street
station the financial district does not quake; clerks,
messengers, and others jostle him about. It is when
he passes through the doors of his bank that his official status appears. The porter bows respectfully.
That is the only salutation which the president feels
bound to return punctiliously. If he should pass
through the whole establishment and into his own
private office without noticing either the cashier, the

vice-president, or his own secretary, that would be no sign of unamiability. He should be thinking in millions. At the door of his room he meditates and stops. The cashier, who is watching from his cage window, wonders who will catch it.

"Henry," says the president to the young man who has a little desk just outside his private door, "that rug ought to be sent out to the cleaner's. It's awful."

"Yes, sir," says Henry.

"Well, send it, then, but first find out how much it will be and let me know."

He disappears into his private office, removes his hat and outer coat, sits down to his desk, picks up the telephone instrument, and the banking day has seriously begun. When the operator answers, he says, "My garage, please," hangs up the receiver, sets the instrument down, and surveys his desk. There is a pile of mail, all opened, and spread out flat, one letter upon another. It looks like a day's work, but he makes short shift of it. The first ten flutter lightly into the waste basket. From the eleventh he unfastens an inclosure and lays it to one side. Three or four more go to the waste basket at a glance, and then one receives a penciled memorandum on the margin. In five minutes he is at the end of them. He pushes a button; a stenographer appears. He hands her the five or six surviving letters, which she takes without comment, and withdraws. The telephone rings, and he takes up the instrument: "John?" It is John, for the president continues. "You say those people want thirty-five dollars for a new crank shaft?

Well, I won't pay it. That's robbery. There's a place over in Newark where you can have one made for eight dollars. Call up Mr. D——'s man and he will tell you where."

As he puts the telephone instrument down he sees his secretary, who lays on his desk some papers and mentions the name of a man who is waiting outside. It is a Wall Street man, with a mind on speculation, who comes now and then prying into the president's thoughts. It is a bother to see him, but he has been useful at times and may be again. "Well, send him in," says the president, and the secretary retires. The man in waiting steps briskly in, with an uneasy manner. "Good-morning," says the president. "Sit down."

A Wall Street man with a speculative mind interviews the president of a great bank awkwardly, and with marked embarrassment. The president of a bank knows everything, from the evening habits of the bank's employees, on up the scale to the moral conduct of the bank's debtors, and, according to the general belief, whether stocks will go up or down. That is what the Wall Street visitor wants to know, but he cannot outright ask. So he says:

"Things look very uncertain to me. I can't get my bearings, especially as to the money market."

That is a safe beginning. One can always talk to a bank president about the money market.

"Things are rather mixed," says the president. "I think, though, the money market is all right."

This leaves the Wall Street man where he started, and he is relieved by an interruption. The secretary, in a low tone, says to the president, "In that matter of disputed interest the man has written again, insisting that he is in the right." The Wall Street man moves as if to withdraw; the president motions him to remain seated, and speaks to the secretary. "You mean about that seven dollars and thirteen cents?" The secretary replies affirmatively, and the president says: "Tell him positively we shall make not the slightest concession. That is final." As the secretary moves away, the president asks: "Did you get an estimate on reglazing that window?" "Yes, sir," replies the secretary. "It is three dollars and fifteen cents." The president is indignant. "That's outrageous. Get some other estimates."

The Wall Street man sees an opening. "People are very extravagant nowadays."

"Extravagant!" says the president. "Why, people are mad. I know of a man who has fifty-six automobiles in his garage. I'd like to know what in the world a man can do with fifty-six cars. I don't see how a man can possibly use more than five."

The Wall Street man cannot see, either. He has only one, and cannot afford that. "What is going to be the outcome of it?" he asks. "It seems to me people cannot go on this way forever. Do you think we have got to have general liquidation?"

"I hardly know what you mean by general liquidation," says the president.

Neither does the Wall Street man. He was only edging his way toward the stock market. He tries again: "Well, doesn't it seem that everything is very high?"

"Some things, no doubt, are high," says the bank president. "It may be that we shall have to have liquidation in some things. Still, this is a very rich country, you must remember."

"Do you think there has been enough liquidation down here?" asks the Wall Street man. By "down here" he means in Wall Street, on the Stock Exchange, in securities, and he has put the question in its least offensive form.

The bank president, who knows perfectly what he means, becomes absorbed in the papers on his desk. He seems about to answer; then he hesitates. Then in a tentative tone he says: "Well—oh—" And the secretary comes in again. "That meeting is at ten-thirty," says the secretary.

"Oh yes; I'd forgotten about it," says the president, rising. The Wall Street man rises, too, and the president, moving toward a door on the other side of the room, says, "Drop in to see me again when you can. I'm always glad to tell you anything."

"Thanks very much," says the Wall Street man. The banker nods his head graciously, the Wall Street man goes out, and one of them is no wiser than before.

# 5

# *The Manipulator*

OF ALL the queer shops in the world, the queerest is that of the manipulator. There is only his name on the door (not always that) unsupported by any connecting legend. If the law required every person to display a sign over his business door it would puzzle the manipulator what to put on his. "Information Utilized to the Highest Advantage." That might answer, unless the law held that a sign should be so comprehensive as to cover the whole of one's business, and in that case something might have to be added in smaller letters like this: "Dealer in Prices, Architect of Markets, Pool Manager, and Consulting Expert."

There is one way in and another way out. Callers never meet. It would embarrass the vice-president of a corporation to meet the president; somebody's private secretary to meet somebody himself; a Tammany Hall politician to meet an Albany statesman, or the cold-footed member of a weak Stock Exchange pool to meet another on the same treacherous errand. They move through the manipulator's shop under safe conduct. Each, as he comes, taps on a little ground-glass door in the outer hall. It opens instantly, as if the man who peers suspiciously out had his hand on it all the time. If the visitor is known, the manipulator is either in or out; if the visitor is unknown, it is uncertain whether such a person as the manipulator ever existed thereabouts, but a card will be taken in. The answer is swiftly returned. Such a person has been found to exist, and is willing presently to see the visitor, if he will "step this way, please," into a room off the hallway.

The contents of this room are inventoried in five minutes. Subscription for the *Financial Chronicle* began in 1893 and was not renewed year before last. *Poor's Manual*, in its green cloth, begins at 1886 and ends at 1901. There are some chairs and two or three vacant desks. The visitor has a quarter of an hour to wonder what the manipulator's room is like, and when at length he is admitted it is disappointing. There is no machinery of manipulation anywhere about. There is a news ticker, overrunning, and a stock ticker in the other corner, but the manipulator never looks at either one. He will ask *you* what the market is doing—whether it is weak or strong. But if you sit with him awhile you get the feeling of machinery somewhere beyond. A door opens quietly and a man approaches the manipulator with a slip of paper. The manipulator reads what is on it and a quiet colloquy occurs: "Did he get this?" "He hasn't reported." "Tell him three more of that." "Yes, sir. What about this other?" "Nothing now."

The machinery of manipulation is in a little mysterious room beyond, and if you should get in you would see very little—nothing more than a row of telephones on the wall, a row of telegraph keys on a shelf, a few chairs to sit on, hooks to hang memoranda on, a stock ticker, a calendar on the wall, and a rug on the floor. These are the essential accessories of manipulation. The telephones run to brokers, and the telegraph wires may run anywhere, and the calendar is very useful. Each manipulator builds his own machine and alone knows how to use it. With messages and with orders to buy and sell he plays upon the telephone and telegraph instruments as a pianist upon his keys.

A successful manipulator is never fat. His eyes are blue or gray; he is vain about his personal appearance. He listens to ideas and delights to meet them with extreme statements. After an expert accountant has entertained him for half an hour with the analytical proof that a certain railroad has been concealing for years its true earning power, he says: "Figures are nothing. They are intended to deceive. I will tell you something. All railroads are potentially bankrupt— all but two or three. They borrow, borrow, borrow, and never redeem a dollar of debt. When a mortgage comes due and the holder of a bond presents himself to ask for the principal, they say, 'Here is another bond.' But he wants his money. 'Well, then, if you insist,' says the railroad, 'wait here a minute, until we can sell this other bond to another man and give you your money.' Analyze that, if you like."

The accountant may be directly followed by a person who brings the manipulator a bear tip on the stock of that same railroad. "So that's what they tell you, do they?" sneers the manipulator. "Did they send you to tell me? No, of course not, but they knew you would. The trouble with your information is that it's wrong. They have concealed the earning power of their property to deceive us—to deceive not me, but the little investors and speculators. I know their figures. The proof is in the figures. The road is earning twenty per cent., and not three or four, as they say, and when they get ready to pay dividends they can." This person thinks the manipulator a great bull, whereas the accountant thought him a bear for all time.

Now comes to the manipulator's shop a persuasive man, an insider, who invites the manipulator to form a pool in the stock of the General Pump Company, whose condition, as he may see from exhibits A, B, and C, in hand, is very promising. They could all go in together, put the stock up twenty points and sell out at a large profit. The manipulator listens wearily and declines. The visitor departs, thinking him a most unresponsive man, but he is no more than outside when the machine in the back office is set in motion, and 2,000 shares of General Pump stock are sold through six brokers, the manipulator ruminating: "If they're so anxious to have me sell their stock for them I think I may sell a little for myself."

A manipulator lets not his right hand know the employment of the left; his employees are unable to tell how he stands on the market. All the employees of a great manipulator once went short of stocks to the utmost of their resources because "the old man" had been selling the market heavily. He probably knew something. They waited for several days for some calamity to happen, but nothing did happen, and presently all the stocks the manipulator had sold began to arrive from London. He had been a large buyer of stock in London before the rise in prices, and nobody but himself knew it. His employees thought he had attacked the market as a bear and had been selling for a decline, whereas he had merely been taking profits. Having taken their losses, they resumed their study of an old "purchase and sale" book containing the record of "the old man's" transactions in ten and twenty share lots years before, when he was broke, seeking therein the secret of his success, which they have never found.

# 6

# The Way of a Client

WHEN A Wall Street man, voluntarily, involuntarily, or on request, tells another Wall Street man what he thinks of the stock market it is understood between them that a statement of opinion, like what brokers call a "G. T. C." order, is only good till canceled, and that it may be canceled without notice. But when a client sits down solemnly with his broker and asks what he shall do with his money, it is different. The same broker who has been giving his "G. T. C." opinions offhand all day runs his fingers through his hair, crosses his legs reflectively, and spars for time.

"You want to know what I really think?"

"Yes, please," says the client.

"You have ten thousand dollars to invest in securities that you can sleep with?"

"Yes."

These exchanges on the broker's part are perfunctory. He is brushing aside the trivialities of Stock Exchange gossip and trying to get hold of his convictions. His client is a man who ought not to speculate. He cannot afford to lose his money.

"Well," says the broker, at length, "I'd advise you for the present to put your money into good bonds. You can buy good bonds to yield—"

"You think this is not a good time to buy stocks?" asks the client, with a note of disappointment.

"I cannot tell you whether stocks will go up or down, temporarily," says the broker. "I can tell you that the future of the stock market is very uncertain. There are times when it is safe to buy good stocks, but just at present the outlook is not clear. Mind you, I am not a prophet."

"Why do you think it is not a good time to buy stocks?"

"Because nobody can say with any degree of assurance what conditions will be like in this country during the next year or two. We have had ten or twelve years of extremely prosperous times, enormous business at very big profits, and several panics from which we have recovered quickly and gone ahead again. People have learned to be extravagant. I doubt if they will economize until they have to, and, until they do begin to economize in earnest, capital cannot be saved in sufficient amounts to finance another great movement forward. Though there has been some liquidation, there is no saying that it is enough. Liquidation, like inflation, may run a good deal further than anybody expects. Some time we shall have to settle down quietly to hard work and saving. It will be postponed as long as possible. It has been postponed once or twice already. It may be postponed again. No one can say for sure. Because people have been so very extravagant they have saved little, and that is why the lender of capital is for the present at an advantage with his surroundings. That is why I advise you to buy bonds. Mind you, again, none of this has anything to do with fluctuations. I am giving you the best advice I can."

"What do you think of Steel common?" the client asks.

"Steel common," says the broker, "is a speculation."

"If business revives it will go up, don't you think?"

"Undoubtedly so," says the broker.

"But you think business will not revive?"

"I have said that the outlook is very uncertain as to general conditions."

"I have a friend who bought Steel common at twelve dollars a share," says the client, tentatively.

"He was very lucky," says the broker.

"Do you think bonds would go up as much as Steel common if business should revive?" asks the client.

"Probably not," says the broker. "In fact, if business should revive in the near future, and begin to boom, bonds might decline."

"How is that?"

"Well, in that case a lot of idle money that has been put into bonds—for instance, by the banks—would be called for in general business, and the banks would sell their bonds."

"But you said a minute ago that there was insufficient capital, and now you talk of idle money," protests the client.

"Yes," says the broker. "Money is not the same thing as capital."

"Why not?"

"Money," says the broker, "is merely a medium of exchange. It expresses current value—the value of capital as well as the value of commodities. But capital really is what people produce over and above what they consume. Capital is labor saved, if you put it so."

"I'm afraid I do not understand," says the client. "These things are beyond me. I wanted something very safe for my money, something I shouldn't have to worry about; but, of course, I should like to buy something that would go up, too."

"Naturally," says the broker. "But a safe investment and a speculative opportunity are rarely combined in the same thing. I have given you my opinion, not on the stock market for a week or a month, but on investment conditions for the next year or two. Your money would be safe in good bonds."

The client will think it over. He thanks the broker, and departs. On the day following, the market advances an average of ½ per cent., Steel being the strongest stock. The broker is called to the telephone. It is the man with the ten thousand, who asks, "Do you feel the same about things as you did yesterday?" The broker patiently replies in the affirmative. Two days later Steel is up 1½ per cent., and the client returns for a second interview. He comments upon the strength of the stock market, and asks, "You feel the same as you did, I suppose?" The broker does. The next day but one Steel common declines 1 per cent., and the general market is weak. The broker is called to the telephone.

It is again the man with the ten thousand, who says: "I believe you are right. You feel just the same, do you?"

The broker answers in the affirmative.

"You see nothing to change your opinion?" the client asks.

"Nothing," says the broker, who leaves the telephone and consults the order clerk. "That man for whom I made up a list of ten bonds—has he given any orders?"

"Yes, sir," answers the order clerk. "He bought one hundred Steel common, fifty Missouri Pacific, fifty Car and Foundry common, and asked me what I thought of Chino."

# 7

# *The Trader*

THE traits and habits of a professional Stock Exchange trader are those of a man who makes money easily, with a minimum of personal discomfort, who must make it before he can lose it, loses it warily, and spends it warm. The stock market is to him the source of all things. He has but to stroke it the right way, and it will yield him anything he can presently wish for; he may happen to stroke it the wrong way and see its teeth, but, by other similes, that is true everywhere and of everything.

An automobile, as the trader thinks of it first, is not a thing on wheels with a horn attachment and soft seats inside; it is 1 or 2 per cent. on 3,000 shares of Union Pacific. What is that? A forenoon's work, with lunch afterward at the broker's invitation. A vacation in Europe is only three or four turns in 500 shares; anybody may do that. True, the market may be ill-humored, and demanding from it a trip to Europe may result in a losing month; but, then, he does not have to go to Europe. If, as is sometimes believed, he has a wife and children and household expenses, a year's rent is 1½ per cent. on 2,000 Steel common. He may be wrong, and take a loss of ⅛ instead, but Steel is still there and contains the rent.

So lives the trader. He wears grooves in the New Street pavement going to and fro between the Stock Exchange floor and the establishment of the only man in the world who knows what a trader's appetite is like. His brokers buy him lunch at midday, dinner up-town at night, and pet him while he is winning. He pretends to scorn them.

He makes his office with the broker who annoys him the least. He arrives at that broker's office a little before ten o'clock and seems never to know what was in the papers. "What do you think of this political situation?" asks the office manager, diffidently. The trader scoffs: "There's no political situation. Look and see if Union doesn't sell *ex* to-morrow." Then he strolls over to the floor and buys 1,000 shares of Reading just to test his feeling of the market. He gets it too easily, or thinks he does, and sells it out instanter. He tries it again, and a third time, and then walks across New Street to think. There he meets another trader, who asks:

"What are you doing?"

"Nothing. You can't bull them. It's no use. This political situation is rotten."

"Are you going to sell them, then?"

"You daren't sell them, either."

Whereon he returns to the floor, trades back and forth in 4,000 or 5,000 shares, evens up all his contracts before three o'clock, and walks off the Exchange, calculating: "Eighth on a thousand, even on two, three-eighths fifteen hundred, even five hundred, less an eighth on two thousand—four thirty-seven fifty. One forty commissions and seventy stamp tax—two hundred and ten from four hundred and thirty-seven fifty. Made two hundred and twenty-seven fifty. Rotten!"

The vocation is purely accidental. There is probably no instance of a young man having been trained up to "beat Stock Exchange fluctuations." Out of three or four generations of brokers' runners a remarkable trader develops. Nobody can account for him. Least of all can he account for himself. There is a Wall Street legend of a meeting between an economic writer who had ably defined the functions of a Stock Exchange trader, and one of the kind in person.

"So you are the professional trader?" said the economist. "Your function, then, is to fill the gap between the seller who seeks a buyer and the buyer who seeks a seller."

"What's that?" asked the trader.

"I am referring," said the writer, "to your economic functions."

"I'm just a trader, trying to beat the game over there."

"Yes, but you have your functions. What do you think of them?"

The trader's suspicions were touched. "You talk like an Englishman," said he. "Here we never say Union Pacifics nor Atchisons—always Union Pacific or Atchison, or whatever it is. Anyhow, I never give tips. I never heard of Functions. They may be good. I trade only in the active stocks."

The limitations of a trader are those of his qualities. He must subsist upon fluctuations; he eats and drinks his profits; his estate is in his pocket. Of a great opportunity in speculation he gets only the forelock. In the first Bryan campaign a Stock Exchange trader who had come up from the Consolidated Exchange and was accounted clever in the pursuit of fractions, amazed his friends by an exhibition of what seemed foolhardy confidence. He bought so many stocks at the low prices that his broker, who was putting the stocks into bank loans, had to report one day that the bank from whom they had been obtaining accommodations would not lend any more money on Stock Exchange collateral unless the payment of its loans was guaranteed to be in gold. "Sure," said the trader. "I'll guarantee to pay them that way. When I have to pay them in gold the bank will be busted." He held his stocks for only a few weeks after the election, took his profit, and was just a trader again. Before the bull market which he had singularly foreseen was half-way over he had lost all of his money fighting the rise. That is what a trader's mind is like.

But he does beat fluctuations. Proof of it is that he survives. The active Stock Exchange traders of to-day are the active traders of five or ten years ago, less the takings of death and a small percentage of loss from impaired efficiency. A trader's going broke is the merest incident. A losing month or two may bring him down to nothing. All that he really loses, in that case, is the pleasure of despising his brokers. One of them will be glad to take him on credit and let him "bang stocks around" in the way he delights to do until he has worked up a credit balance. He is a prized source of commissions. These are either $1, $2, or $3.25 per 100 shares, according to the way of handling the account, and though this seems small as compared with $12.50 which the outsider pays, it mounts up rapidly with the prodigious quantity of stocks a seasoned trader will deal in. One trader was known to pay in a single year $20,000 in transfer taxes. That represented transactions in 1,000,000 shares.

Absurdly small though the trader's profits be in proportion to the volume of his trading, his losses are smaller still. He has the gambler's instinct for keeping percentages in his favor. He is the only person in Wall Street who, without putting anything into the market, takes his living out of it.

# 8

# *The Invisibles*

A PROFESSIONAL speculator who never was known to put up margins, and an option dealer who paid his commissions and interest in advance in cash, had mingled their sighs and were staring silently at the tape, when the broker approached and introduced between them a message from the floor of the Stock Exchange—warm off the wire. It bore only the initial of the member who had sent it. The message was:

"They are selling this Union Pacific."

It seemed to annoy the speculator. "Whom does he mean by they?" he asked. "*They* do this, *they* do that, *they* are selling stocks. Why can't a man say whom he means? That's the kind of talk you hear in New Street. It's they and they and they until one must be sick of it. They put the market up or they put the market down, or, to be more absurd, they are going to put the market up or down. A man just stopped me in New Street to tell me he feared *they* were filling *him* up with stocks."

"Well," said the broker, "you needn't take me up so. I didn't write the message. I only showed it to you. It does look as if somebody were selling Union Pacific."

That seemed to annoy the speculator more. "Of course it looks as if somebody were selling Union Pacific," he said, scornfully. "That's the illusion. How much Union Pacific have you in this office?"

"I think we haven't any Union Pacific long on balance," said the broker.

"I know you haven't," said the speculator. "Commission houses have no Union Pacific, no Reading, no Steel, not any of the active stocks. It looks as if somebody were selling stocks, and yet we know of nobody who has any stocks to sell. I haven't any. You haven't any. Your clients haven't any. The sellers, therefore, are buying from themselves."

"You seem to be bullish," said the broker. "What do you base it on?"

"It's no use telling you," said the speculator. "You'd tear every bull argument to pieces. When money is cheap and commission houses haven't any stocks, one has got to stop his ears and close his eyes and be bullish—just because. You say it looks as if somebody were selling Union Pacific. So it does. Therefore, I don't look at it. The only way to make money in this market is to be bullish—because. The manipulation is always new. As people learn the old tricks, new tricks have to be invented. Do you recall how hard it was to bull stocks in 1904? Then their tactics were to churn one or two stocks at a time, without changing prices any to speak of. There would be one hundred and fifty thousand shares of Pennsylvania one day, four hundred thousand shares of Reading the next, and so on through the list, over and over, and yet there was no business. Brokers were doing nothing. Now they are pursuing tactics which are new and equally misleading. They take one or two stocks at a time and buy them. They buy fifteen thousand or twenty thousand shares, and then they stop. Prices react two or three points, and if you have bought the same stocks you are disgusted and let go. Then they go in and buy them again. They already have all the stocks. They are now buying all the contracts anybody will sell on the short side. I've seen it."

"Whom do *you* mean by they?" the broker asked.

"He's referred to them ten times," said the option dealer. "I counted him as he went along."

"You may laugh," retorted the speculator. "You know perfectly well whom I mean. I am referring to the invisible buyers. They are the same as the invisible sellers at the top of a bull market. What do you see then? Everywhere you go people are buying stocks. You never hear of a man selling anything. Who are the sellers? They exist, but they are invisible. Your telephones are hot. One client wants five hundred Northern Pacific. An invisible seller accommodates him. Another wants three hundred St. Paul, and another invisible seller attends to him. You can't send the orders so fast but the invisible sellers will fill them. One hundred of this, please, and there you are; fifteen hundred of that, please, and here you are; three hundred of something else, quick, and quick it is. Then, when prices are away down, it's the other way. The invisibles are the buyers. Wherever you go, people are selling something. One says to please sell him one hundred Steel common, because the steel business is so rotten, and it comes out on the tape—sold, one hundred Steel common, for the account of your client. Who bought it? Another says please to sell for him one thousand St. Paul, because it is going to pass its dividend, and an invisible buyer takes it. I don't know who those invisible sellers and buyers are; I can only guess. I know they exist, and that it's bad practice to sell when they buy, or to buy when they sell. I attach great importance to what the invisible man does."

A boy brought the broker another message. It bore the same initial as the first one. The broker passed it to the speculator. "I asked R. L. to say whom he meant by they, and this is what he answers."

The message read: "Union Pacific is being sold steadily by the people you never see, and whose orders you cannot trace. They sell it on every strong spot."

The speculator was quiet for a moment. Then he said: "He may be right. Nobody can tell. But when

Union is two hundred he will tell you *they* are buying it."

He passed out of the office and into the street, and met a manipulator with whom he was on friendly terms.

"Well," asked the manipulator, "what do they say around?"

"They say you are a great bear on the market," answered the speculator. He had heard no such thing; but he wished to draw the manipulator out.

"They say anything," replied the manipulator, wearily. "I'm not doing anything in the market at all. They tell me the steel business is in a desperate way, that dividends will have to be cut, that labor has got to be liquidated, and that the bond market is manipulated. I notice, though, that they are not selling stocks."

The manipulator was on his way to call on a great private banker, who asked: "Well, what do you know?"

"They say I'm a bear on the market," said the manipulator, "but really I'm nothing. By the way, what are they going to do with that Reading?"

"I've heard many stories," said the banker, "but I don't know. They may know themselves, but nobody else does. Possibly they don't know themselves."

The third person invisible in Wall Street is wiser than all the rest.

# 9

# *A Real Inside View*

ABOUT a large private banking house in Wall Street there is an air of omniscience as if nothing unexpected could ever happen. Doors do not slam, men walk softly upon rugs, voices are never lifted in feverish excitement over profit and loss; no one is permitted even to call off prices from the tape. There is first a feeling of space, quite different from that sense of limited margins which pervades a broker's office. Ceilings in a banking house are higher than ceilings anywhere else, and that may account for it, but even before one is conscious of dimensions one gets the feeling of space from the manners of the person in uniform who attends to the noiseless opening and closing of the main portal and asks people what business they have to enter.

The responsibilities of private banking rest much more visibly upon this individual than upon the partners. He rules over all that probationary space lying between the entrance and the marble railing at which any trivial business may be transacted, and beyond which all important business must take place. One may see over. Nothing is concealed, not even the great bankers. Their degrees of greatness (or perhaps only their degrees of seniority) are known by the position of their desks.

The junior partner has the desk nearest the marble railing and most exposed to the scrutiny of all comers. The one of next greatness has the desk next farther removed, and so it goes, up to the senior partner, sometimes known reverentially in the back office as the "old man." His desk is at the big window. He himself is almost invisible; he is visible or invisible at will. Each partner's name is at the end of his desk on a brass plate. Why that is nobody ever knew. They certainly know each other; all the employees know them apart. No visitor is ever admitted to go wandering to and fro among the desks, looking for a man by his name-plate. It was probably an idea of the desk-makers.

When momentous things are forward, the atmosphere may be one of restrained expectancy, in which everybody shares to the degree of his station, though without being in the least excited; but on the afternoon of a thin December day of a year like 1910 in Wall Street there is nothing conceivably more restful than the omniscient certainty that nothing at all is going to happen. One partner may be observed in the labor of composition. It is not a business letter, or he would be dictating it to a stenographer, and, besides, the business letters of banking firms are not written on monogram stationery. The junior partner suddenly leaves off poking the insides of a costly thin timepiece with a pearl-handled letter-opener, snaps the case shut, holds his left waistcoat pocket open wide, and tosses the watch in (as if it were a trick); he thrusts both hands deep in his trousers pockets, and strolls softly over to the ticker.

Nobody has been at the ticker for the last half-hour; the tape has overrun the basket, and is piling itself up on the floor. He coaxes it back in the way it should go, stares at the world outside, strolls back to his desk, considers its orderly condition, and then comes up behind a clerk who has a desk (without a name-plate) hard up against the marble railing.

Just then the great door is pushed open by a man of business, who waives the uses of the man in uniform, leans over the marble railing and says to the clerk:

"Three-eighths is my limit."

"I refused that over the telephone five minutes ago," says the clerk.

"Then we can't trade?"

"Only at three-quarters."

The man of business goes out. "What's that?" asks the junior partner. "Those A. & R. debentures," says the clerk.

"Ah!" says the junior partner, shrewdly. All that he has contributed to this great banking business is his inherited capital and a knowing way of saying "Oh!"

A round person, containing great potentialities of noise, comes in with some visible constraint. The man in uniform makes as if to open the door, but allows the round person to admit himself. He turns around twice—all around—and says to the man in uniform: "Is Mr. X—— busy?" "He is busy," says the man in uniform. "Won't Mr. D—— do?" "Mr. D—— will not do; but, anyhow, it was nothing very important, if everybody is busy," and the round person retires. He was a broker, on an aimless errand. He is hardly gone when the man in uniform moves attentively to the door and opens it wide for an elderly, abrupt man. He is the president of a corporation, who has been unable to agree with the "old man" as to the terms of certain financing. He broke off negotiations an hour ago. The "old man" mentioned it to his most active partner, who told another partner, who told the junior partner, who told the clerk, who told the man in uniform, so that everybody knew the deal was off.

"Has there been a telegram for me?"

"No, sir," answers the man in uniform. As the corporation president turns to go, he adds: "I'm very sorry, sir."

The corporation president looks at him, as if he would say, "Sorry for what?" and departs. That was all he had come back for—a telegram. The letter-writing partner, who has been listening, yawns.

The "old man" and two partners are intimately engaged in conversation. "The trouble with giving them as much as last year, besides the cost of it," the senior is saying, "is that it establishes a kind of minimum. I don't like that. If there is anything in the Christmas bonus custom at all, the distribution ought to be proportionate to the year's profits. Then there is, of course, the other difficulty. It will become known what bonus we give; it may even get published in the newspapers, and if we give less than last year it will advertise the fact that we have had an unprofitable season. It's all nonsense—the whole thing. I have no doubt that down the street they will give their employees more than last year, in order to create the impression that they have had a prosperous year. I know they haven't."

"Couldn't we give them stock in something instead of money?" asks one of the partners.

The "old man" looks at him, pityingly, gets up, calls for his hat and coat, and a December banking day is closed.

# 10

# *The Wall Street Wolf*

IN THE Wall Street district are many coyotes and a wolf. One wolf is enough. One is an institution. He is useful to those greater animals, the bulls and the bears; and useful at times to the police, and gains thereby the immunity and toleration which are so useful to himself. You may observe him in New Street, always moving, always' tending on his way, never stopping to waste his time in mere chatter with other mammals. He wears expensive clothes, often a silk hat, carries a stick, and delights to feel that he is pointed out. Even a wolf may be proud of it. The thing that bulges his coat pocket out is a copy of the Penal Code. He carries it always.

Several years ago the wolf made himself useful to the New York police in a very odd way. Some one had forged a certified check and had got the money; it was a considerable amount, and there was no clue to the criminal. After many days of futile activity the police thought to consult the wolf. A man who was morally known to have committed so many villainies without once having betrayed himself into the hands of the law was worth consulting. And this was a matter pretty much in his own line. It was a crime against money. The wolf is a man who has so perfected that sort of industry that he becomes respected; the police admire his subtlety. They asked him to help catch the forger. He asked to see the forged check. Across the face of a certified check is stamped the word "Certified" or "Accepted." The wolf looked at this check for a minute, handed it back to the police, and said:

"Find the man who made the rubber-stamp."

The police started at once on the rubber-stamp makers, located the one who had made this particular stamp, and got their first clue to the forger. A few hours later he was in jail.

The wolf himself would never be guilty of forgery. He is too careful for that. He observes the Penal Code. He uses his head. He particularly delights to catch a marauding bull or bear making off stealthily with rich booty. He puts himself across such an animal's way or pursues him, demanding a share of the booty. He is a wolf, and no hog, and knows what a decent share is, but unless he gets it he will raise an outcry. He will, for instance, bring what in Wall Street is called a "strike suit." He will appear as an injured stockholder and enjoin a great corporation from doing a thing which the insiders, perhaps, are selfishly bent upon doing. Then there will be publicity, notoriety, difficulties of all sorts, and it had been cheaper to give the wolf his share.

If there were many wolves the other animals, bulls and bears, would have to drop everything else and unite to exterminate them, but one wolf has protection. He can be employed. It sometimes happens that bulls fall out, perhaps over so simple a thing as arithmetic, that is, long division, and that one who thinks he has been cheated would like very much to harry another, only he dares not attempt it openly. Then he sends for the wolf, who brings the suit which the disappointed bull could not bring in his own name. After that there are two to be settled with—the wolf and his principal. The wolf receives and divides, and he divides fair, because, unless he were helpful and trustworthy in these things, he could not expect protection.

Once a number of Wall Street speculators were in a pool together and thought they had cornered a certain stock. One of their number was manager of the pool; he was a great manipulator. Presently things began to go wrong. Nobody understood it, least of all the manipulator's associates in the pool. Stock kept coming continually upon the market for sale, and the pool had to go on buying it to keep the price up. The mystery was where the stock came from. The manipulator was suspected, but nothing could be proved. He had been known before to sell out on his associates. At length two of them set a watch upon him, and one evening late he was discovered in earnest conference with the wolf. That was quite enough. The spies understood perfectly that the manipulator, wishing to sell out and not be suspected, had called the wolf to his assistance. The wolf, well provided with margin money, had opened accounts with many brokers and was selling the stock short for the manipulator who loaned the pool's stock for delivery on short contracts.

The wolf has done some amazing things out of sheer, uncontrollable impudence. Once, when negotiations to settle a big coal miners' strike had finally failed, because the representatives of both sides were too stiff-necked to meet, and had been unable to accomplish anything by proxy, the wolf took up the telephone and called the banker who represented the railroad companies. Without giving his name, he said that he represented the president of the miners' association, who wished to know if the banker would see him personally. It was such an overture as saved the banker's pride, and he consented. Then the wolf called the president of the miners' association on the telephone, and said, speaking for the banker, that the banker wished to see him in person. That was an overture to save the labor leader's pride. Two more telephone calls, one each way, and a meeting was definitely arranged. The wolf thereupon withdrew, and perhaps made some money on the rise in prices which followed the settlement of the strike forty-eight hours later.

No great Wall Street personages can afford to be seen publicly with the wolf, or even to recognize him in the street, but more of them know him and are known to him than you would easily believe. He once presented to a man of finance a proposition which from any other source must have been alluring. The man said to the wolf:

"You yourself have a bad reputation. Whom can you bring to convince me of your sincerity?"

Instead of naming persons whom he might have induced to come, the wolf, taking a dramatic risk, said, "Any man you name."

The man mentioned the most unlikely person he could think of. "Then," said he, "bring Russell Sage."

And the wolf brought him. These things are not to be too definitely accounted for.

No office, no address, has the wolf. He lives in his audacity, which is capacious, and subsists upon the follies and fears and credulities—not of the lambs, who are the common prey, but of Wall Street people, who, of all the people in the world, the wolf thinks, are the silliest, the afraidest, the most credulous and gullible, if you only know them.

# 11

# *Taking Trouble Home*

A T THE end of a day badly spent in Wall Street a married man affects to dine, and then he smokes and revolves the problem that when one wins money one wins such a little, though when one loses one loses a lot. Such train of thought is not conducive to good domestic conversation, and is rudely broken in upon:

"You have not spoken ten words since you entered the house. You ate very little dinner. Aren't you well?"

"I'm all right, I guess; only I wasn't very hungry," the man answers.

"Did you bring the papers home?"

"No. I read them on the train, and threw them away."

"Was there anything in them?"

"There never is."

The reason why winning money is like putting mustard seeds one at a time in a bag, while losing it is like bursting the bag, is that—

"What did the market do to-day?"

"It was weak."

"Very weak?"

"Yes."

"How much did it go down?"

"My dear, how can one say how much the market went up or down? The market is made up of many stocks. They all go up and down. Do you want to know about any particular stock?"

"No; of course not. You know I'm not interested in any particular stock. But can't you tell me about how much the market went down?"

"Oh, three to ten points."

"Were you—what is it?—were you short of stocks?"

"No."

"It seems to me you are never short of stocks when the market goes down. Can't one see that the market is going down?"

"No, my dear, not always."

"What caused the market to go down?"

"The Interstate Commerce Commission refused to allow the railroads to raise their rates. It came out—the decision did—after the close of the market yesterday, and took everybody by surprise."

"Did you think the railroads would be allowed to raise their rates?"

"Of course I did. I wouldn't have been such a fool as to stay long of stocks if I hadn't thought so."

"Why did you think that?"

"Why? That's an idle question. Everybody thought so."

"I've often heard you say that what everybody thinks is sure to be wrong in the stock market."

"You don't understand these things. I wish you wouldn't worry about them."

Again, the reason why losing money is like letting the bag burst is that—

"I knew the Interstate Commerce Commission, or whatever it is, wouldn't allow the railroads to raise their rates."

"You knew it! Will you be so good as to tell me how you knew it?"

"Why, it's very simple. By rates you mean what the railroads get for hauling things, don't you?"

"Yes."

"It is what the railroads earn?"

"Yes."

"Well, after all you have told me about railroad earnings being greater than ever before, and dividends the highest the railroads ever were able to pay, I should have known that they wouldn't be allowed to raise their rates. Why should they be?"

"Why, because—although their earnings—that is, their net earnings—I mean— Oh, what's the use to talk about it? You wouldn't know what I was talking about."

Is it not the very—well, whatever it is a man cannot say it out loud, and it does no good to say it mentally. Still, a man may think. But he may not think,
either, with a woman pestering his head off. A man
who gets his money in Wall Street ought to live in a
cave. He does his best, which is bad enough, and
would like to leave it all behind him down-town, but
no! The woman must have it all over again, in her
silly way. Does she not get enough to eat? Does she
not get her gowns and her luxuries, whether the
market goes up or down? What more can she expect? Does she think she helps by this? A man may
think himself a fool, but he does not like his wife so
good as to call him one. Is it not—

"Has my investment done anything?"

"What investment?"

"There! That's what I might have expected. You
come home and tell me you have made an investment for me. You tell me not to ask any questions—
not to ask even the name of the stock, but that when
it turns out as you think you will give me the money.
Naturally, I am curious about it. I haven't mentioned
it since, though that was three months ago, and now
I merely ask you how it is getting on, and you snap at
me like that."

"Pooh, now. Never mind. I'm a little bit crusty
this evening. Your investment is all right. It's a little
slower than I thought it would be, but it will turn out
all right. It will buy you all the gowns you want next
winter."

A man is a beast. He ought not to be such a beast. He ought to allow for the fact that a woman naturally is interested in what a man is doing, though she cannot understand. A man ought to be sorry for all the ugly things he says. He ought to—

"Not till next winter?"

"Well, I'm giving it plenty of time."

"But things are going up and down all the time. Yesterday I saw in the paper that one stock had advanced fifteen points in one day. Why couldn't you have had that?"

"That was some inactive thing—Lackawanna or American Express; something that nobody ever trades in."

"It was Lackawanna. I noticed it particularly. I had been thinking that Lackawanna would go up."

"Why?"

"Well, I just thought it ought to. It always does go up that way. Are you short of the market now, or long of it?"

"I'm short of it."

"I should think after a break of three to ten points it would be a good time to buy stocks. I think the market will go up."

"Why?"

"Doesn't it always go up after it has gone down a lot?"

"Madam, if you will be so good as to mind your business I will mind mine. Now let that suffice."

The market went up.

# *Anatomy*
# *of the Bubble*

The following article, "Anatomy of the Bubble," was published in *A Bubble That Broke the World* in 1932. Most of the material in that book appeared in the *Saturday Evening Post* between May 1931 and May 1932. In the collection of articles Garrett focuses on a certain type of bubble—not one formed by a mania or "irrational exuberance," but a less visible bubble created and subsequently kept afloat by debt. Whether pertinent to today's market or not, it is an insightful examination of bubbles in general. Eerily, it almost foreshadows World War II.

*Who, then, is he who provides it all? Go and find him and you will have once more before you The Forgotten Man.* . . . *The Forgotten Man is delving away in patient industry, supporting his family, paying his taxes, casting his vote, supporting the church and the school, reading his newspaper, and cheering for the politician of his admiration, but he is the only one for whom there is no provision in the great scramble and the big divide.*

—WILLIAM GRAHAM SUMNER

Command of labor and materials built the pyramids. The economic world was then very simple. Some private usury, of course, but no banking system, no science of credit, no engraved securities issued on the pyramids for investors to worry about. Merely, the whim of Pharaoh, his idea of a pyramid, his power to move labor, and the fact of a surplus of food enough to sustain those who were diverted from agriculture to monumental masonry.

It is believed that on Cheops alone 100,000 men were employed for twenty years. And when it was finished all that Egypt had to show for 600,000,000 days of human labor was a frozen asset. Otherwise and usefully employed, as, for example, upon habitations and hearthstones, works of common utility, means of national defense, that amount of labor might have raised the standard of common living in Egypt to a much higher plane, besides insuring Egyptian civilization a longer competitive life. But once it had been spent on a pyramid to immortalize the name of Pharaoh it was spent forever. People could not consume what their own labor had produced. That is to say, they could not eat a pyramid, or wear it, or live in it, or make any use of it whatever. Not even Pharaoh could sell it, rent it, or liquidate it.

History does not say what happened to the 100,000 when Cheops was finished. Were they unemployed? Were they returned to agriculture whence they came? If so, that would be like now sending suddenly four or five million people from industry back to the farms in this country.

You may take it, at any rate, that when Cheops was finished, there occurred in Egypt what we should call an economic crisis, with no frightful statistics, no collapsing index numbers in the daily papers, no stock-exchange panic, no bank failures, but with unemployment, blind social turmoil, Egyptian bread lines perhaps. And this crisis, like every crisis since, down to the very last, was absorbed by people who could not consume what they had produced, whose labor had been devoured by a pile of stones, and who understood it dimly if at all. The forgotten people.

This story of a pyramid has the continuing verity of a parable. For all the worlds that have passed since that Egyptian civilization departed, for all the new wonders of form, method and power that seem to make this one of ours original, nevertheless, what happened to the forgotten people of Egypt happens still in our scheme; it happens to The Forgotten Man of William G. Sumner's classic essay, and for the same reasons.

There is here no solitary Pharaoh with the power to move labor by word alone. In this world labor is free, receiving wages. Yet you have to see that the passion among us for individual and collective aggrandizement by command of labor and materials is what it always was and that the consequences of pursuing it far in selfish and uneconomic ways are what they are bound to be and anciently were.

In place of one responsible Pharaoh at a time, we have a multitude of irresponsible Pharaohs; and beyond these we have the Pharaoh passion acting in governments big and little, in States and cities, in great private and public organizations, all seeking their own exaggeration and all seeking it by the one means. The motive may be avarice, it may be good or bad, it may derive from a sense of rivalry between nations or from an idea of public happiness. In the nature of economic consequences, strange to say, the motive does not matter. A pyramid is a pyramid still. When too much labor has been spent upon pyramids, or things that are unproductive and dead in the economic meaning of pyramids, there will be a crisis in daily well-being, and free labor in that case will be as helpless as slave labor was. It cannot consume what it has produced; it is without all those human satisfactions that might have been produced with the same labor in place of the pyramid, and it is without them forever. The labor that is lost cannot be recovered by unbuilding the pyramid.

But in this world where labor is free and no one has the apparent power to move it beyond its own volition, how is it moved or procured to waste itself too far upon works of public and private aggrandizement? How now do we build pyramids? There is a new way. It is a way the ancients, the Pharaohs, with no science of banking, could not have imagined. The name of it is credit. In our world, a world of money economy, command of credit is the command of labor and materials. There may be intervening complexities, the obvious may be obscured, yet in every case that is what it comes to at last; and, in fact, people have no other use for credit.

Borrowing and lending are as old as the sense of mine and thine; therefore, so is credit in the simple term. But modern credit as we know it, or think we know it, is a new and amazing power, still evolving, still untamed. Men have been much more anxious to release the power of credit, to employ and exploit it, than to control it or even to understand it. That would be only human. As formerly there was no aggrandizement, private or public, without a Pharaoh-like command of labor and materials, so now there is none without command of credit.

This holds for aggrandizement in any dimension. The very magnitude of human life in the present earth is owing to the power of credit. The whole of our industrial phenomena is founded on it. By means of credit the machine is created in the first place; by means of credit the machine is manned and moved and fed with raw materials. By means of credit the product of machines is distributed. By means of credit more and more this product is consumed, as when credit is loaned at home to the instalment buyer or loaned abroad to the foreign customer. Thus the power of credit is employed dynamically in the aggrandizement of trade, wherein are many dangers yet to be explored, such as those of wild inflation and deflation, followed by sudden crisis. The greed of individuals and groups, the extravagances of civic ego, the ambition of nations, ideas creative and destructive both, great social ends and great fallacies at the same time, even war—credit for all of these is the fabulous agent. And then, besides, with any motive, it builds pyramids, which is the singular point and the one we are after.

That is the one thing credit is supposed not to do. The restraining principles are interest and amortization. To amortize a debt is to redeem it, to extinguish it finally, or, literally, put it to death. Debt we have not mentioned. Most of the follies we commit with the power of credit are from forgetting that debt is the other face of credit. There is no credit but with an exact equivalent of debt. That is to say, when by means of credit you command labor and materials, you borrow them and become a debtor. As a debtor you must pay interest, so much per annum, on what you have borrowed, and sometime later return the principal, which puts the debt to death. We suppose commonly that interest and amortization concern only the borrower and lender. Who lends money will demand something for the use of it while he himself is doing without it, and surety for its return after a certain time. That is so; but that is not all of it.

From the point of view of the total social organism, interest and amortization have a kind of functional significance. They are the only two checks we have upon the universal passion to abuse the power of credit, or to waste in reckless and uneconomic ways the labor that is by credit commanded.

The borrower is expected to say: "This thing I propose to create with credit will be in turn creative. I mean it will be productive and give increase. Out of the increase I will pay interest for use of the credit; out of the increase I will extinguish the debt. The remainder I will keep for my own as profit."

He may say that of a steel works, a textile factory, a railroad, an electric-power plant, of ten thousand and one things you may not think of; he cannot say it of a pyramid.

Precisely, therefore, the function of interest and amortization, beyond any private concern of either borrower or lender, is to restrain pyramid building. Nevertheless, it will be perceived that the modern world is magnificent with pyramids. Where Pharaoh built one by tyrannical command of labor and materials, credit now builds thousands. You are not to look for them in the exact shape of Pharaoh's. Ours are in shapes of endless variety, many of them apparent, some not so apparent because they present a specious aspect of usefulness, and some invisible. The invisible kind are of all the most devouring.

Taking them by kinds, what are they—our pyramids? The most obvious to perception are those in the category of public works, such as monumental buildings, erections to civic grandeur, ornate boulevards, stadiums, recreation centers, communal baths, and so on. Here, to begin with, the restraining function of interest and amortization is relaxed. It is not said that works in this character will be productive. It is said that they will contribute to the happiness and comfort of people, which is their justification, and it is generally true. And it is said, moreover: "Why should people wait until they can have saved the money for this extension of their happiness and comfort when they may have it immediately on credit? They will tax themselves to pay interest on the debt and to pay the principal of the debt as it comes due."

But so even with pyramids in this very desirable meaning, let the impatience for them become extravagant and reckless, as it will and does, and let too much labor be moved by credit to the making of them all at once, and you may be sure of what will happen. To pay interest on the debt and then to pay the debt itself taxes will rise until people cannot afford to pay them. That is what they will say. But the reason they cannot afford to pay taxes is that they could not afford those very desirable unproductive things to begin with. Either they did not know this in time or they did not care. They may repudiate the debt, yet as you may consider society in the whole that will make no difference whatever, since it remains true that society in the whole is wanting all those other exchangeable human satisfactions, more important than sights and diversions, that might have been produced with the same labor in place of those well-intentioned and premature pyramids.

In another category are things that afterward turn into pyramids. This will happen when those by whom the credit was commanded have used it with bad judgment, or too much of it for a given result, or dishonestly, or to create a thing for which after all there is no demand, so that what they were pursuing was not a reality within reason of probability but a delusion of profit—and pursuing it with other people's labor, other people's money. Yet the thing itself may be magnificent, like the tallest skyscraper in a great city, so marvellous in its architectural and engineering features that people will come from great distances away for the thrill of looking at it. Whether or not in such a case given, the entire motive was profit, free of any will to aggrandizement, it is profit or loss that will determine the economic status of each new piece of wonder. If there is profit, if it can pay interest and put the debt to death out of its earnings, or, that is to say, if it can return to the common reservoir the credit that was borrowed, then it is not a pyramid. It is a thing productive, giving increase. But if there is loss, so that interest and amortization cannot be met out of the increase, out of the earnings, out of the rents, then and exactly in the measure to which this is true, the thing is a pyramid. We say in that case the capital is lost. But what the loss of capital means is that the labor is lost, and again, no matter who specifically takes the loss, society as a whole is wanting all the imaginable other satisfactions that might have been produced in place of this pyramid.

By the same definition, the overbuilding of industry beyond any probable demand for the product represents devoured credit. Here the spirit of aggrandizement acts as if it were a biological law, each separate organization trying to outgrow all the others of its own kind in the industry of one country, and then that industry as a whole in one country trying to outgrow the competitive industry of another country, and this going on with benefit of more and more credit, until at last—what is the problem? The problem is that so much credit, that is to say labor, is trapped, frozen, locked up in the world's industrial machine, that people cannot afford to buy the whole of its product at prices which will enable industry to pay interest on its debt. This is perhaps the most involved form of pyramid that human ingenuity has yet devised.

To see it clearly, you may have to push it to the focus of extreme absurdity. Suppose, for example, that half of all the capital in the world were invested in shoe-making machinery. You have there the capacity to make in one day many more shoes than there are feet in the world, and yet the necessity to pay interest on half the capital in the world and charge it to the price of shoes will make shoes so dear that nobody can afford to buy them. The answer is that all the capital invested in excess shoe-making machinery is lost. Nearly half the capital in the world! Half less the relatively small amount that may be properly so invested. Exactly. It is really lost. The labor it represents is lost. All the wanted things that this labor might have produced in place of that excess of shoe-making machinery—they are lost, and forever lost. You cannot recover the labor by unbuilding the machinery any more than Pharaoh could have recovered his wasted Egyptian labor by unbuilding the pyramid.

Then the invisible pyramids—what are they?

A delirious stock-exchange speculation such as the one that went crash in 1929 is a pyramid of that character. Its stones are avarice, mass-delusion and mania; its tokens are bits of printed paper representing fragments and fictions of title to things both real and unreal, including title to profits that have not yet been earned and never will be. All imponderable. An ephemeral, whirling, upside-down pyramid, doomed in its own velocity. Yet it devours credit in an uncontrollable manner, more and more to the very end; credit feeds its velocity.

In two years brokers' loans on the New York Stock Exchange alone increased five billions of dollars. That was credit borrowed by brokers on behalf of speculators, and it was used to inflate the daily Stock

Exchange quotations for those bits of printed paper representing fragments and fictions of title to things both real and unreal. It was credit that might have been used for productive purposes. The command of labor and materials represented by that amount of credit would have built an express highway one hundred feet wide from New York to San Francisco and then one from Chicago to Mexico City, with something over. Or taking wages at six dollars a day, it represents more than the six hundred million days of man power wasted by Pharaoh on his Cheops. But the use of it to inflate Stock Exchange prices added not one dollar of real wealth to the country.

You may think that since it was all a delusion on the profit side, the loss also must have been imaginary; that if nothing was added to the wealth of the country, neither was anything taken away. But that is not the way of it. First there was the direct loss of diverting that credit from all the possible uses of production to the unproductive use of speculation. Secondly, a great deal of it was consumed by two or three million speculators, large and small, who, with that rich feeling upon them, borrowed money on their paper profits and spent it. In this refinement of procedure what happens is that imaginary wealth is exchanged for real wealth; and the real wealth is consumed by those who have produced nothing in place of it. Thirdly—and this was the terrific loss—the shock from the headlong fall of this pyramid caused all the sensitive sources and streams and waters of credit to contract in fear. The more they contracted the more fear there was, the more fear the more contraction, effect acting upon cause. The sequel was abominable panic.

This is only the most operatic example of the pyramid invisible. Such a thing must be any artificial or inflated price structure, requiring credit to support it. The Federal Farm Board built two great pyramids in agriculture, one in wheat and one in cotton, and named them stabilization. It was using government credit, borrowed from the people, to support wheat and cotton prices. Nevertheless, wheat and cotton prices were bound to fall, and that credit was lost. There has been a vogue for pyramids by the name of stabilization. Scores of them have been built, private and public, all using credit in a more or less desperate effort to support prices that were bound for natural reasons to fall.

Foreign trade inflated by the credit we loaned to our foreign customers—that was a grand pyramid of a special kind, half visible and half invisible, partly real and partly unreal. The trade was visible; the idea of profit in it was largely a delusion. Almost we forgot that we were buying this trade with our own credit.

Moreover, of total loans out of the American credit reservoir to foreign countries, amounting grossly to fifteen billions of dollars, a great deal of it has been used not to inflate foreign trade but by the foreign borrowers to build pyramids of their own at our expense. This magnificent oddity, here only to be mentioned, will return in its due place.

A certain confusion may now be beginning to rise. Credit, again, regarded simply as a command of labor and materials. In that definition the mind makes no difficulty about relating it to ponderable things, such as pyramids in the form of public works or excess industrial capacity, for these are only certain physical objects in place of others that might have been wrought with the instrumentality of that same credit; it may, however, find some difficulty in relating it to imponderable things also called pyramids, such as a Wall Street ecstasy. For how does credit originate? Whose is it to begin with? How is command of it acquired? How does it get from where it originates to where it is found producing its prodigious effects?

All of this may be seen, and will be easier to do than you would think. To see credit rising at its source, to see whose it is to begin with, to see how it moves from the spring to the stream and then anywhere, even to the maelstrom, and to see at the same time Sumner's Forgotten Man, you have only to go to the nearest bank and sit there for half an hour in an attitude of attention. Any bank will do. The first one you come to.

Observe first the physical arrangements. There will be along the counter a series of little windows, each with a legend over it. Above one window it will be "Savings." Over the next two or three it will be "Teller." Then one, "Discounts and Collections." And at one side, where the counter ends, you will see behind a railing several desks with little metal plates on them, one saying "President," another "Vice President," and another "Cashier," unless it is a very small bank, in which case the cashier will be behind one of the windows.

Then observe the people and what they come to do. Some go straight to the window marked "Savings." These all bring money to leave with the bank at interest. One is a man in overalls. That is wage money to be saved. Another is a farmer's wife, and that may be milk or butter money. Next the poultry man with some profit to be put aside. Then two or three housewives, evidently, such as regularly include in their budgets a sum to be saved. After these a foreman from the railroad and a garage mechanic, and so on. Each one puts money between the leaves of a little book and pushes it through the window; the man there counts it, writes the amount in the little book and pushes the book back to the depositor. That goes on all day. At the day's end all the money received at this window is counted, bundled and tossed into the safe, and then written down in the big book of the bank as "Time Deposits."

Those who go to the windows marked "Teller" are somewhat different. They represent local trade, commerce and industry. Their accounts are current, called checking accounts or credit balances. They bring both cash and checks to deposit; and besides making deposits they may tender their own checks to be cashed, often at the same time. For example, the man who owns the sash and blind factory brings nothing but checks to deposit; everybody owing him money has paid him by check. But he hires ten men and this is pay day. Therefore, needing cash to pay wages, he writes his own check for the amount of his pay roll and receives that sum in cash. But this money he takes away presently comes back to the bank through other hands. The employees of the sash and blind factory spend it with the grocer and butcher and department-store keeper who immediately bring it to the bank and deposit it at the "Teller" windows where it came from. What the employees of the sash and blind factory do not spend they themselves bring back to the bank and leave at the window marked "Savings." Such is the phenomenon called the circulation of money. The same dollar may go out of the bank and return again two or three times in one week. The speed with which a dollar performs its work and returns to the bank is called the velocity of money.

At the end of the day the men at the "Teller" windows count up in one column what they have received and in another what they have paid out, and the difference is written down in the bank's books as an increase or decrease of "Demand Deposits." The rule is that more will have been received than was paid out, so there is normally each day an increase of deposits. It is normal that all these people representing local business should bring to the "Teller" windows more than they take away, because their activities are severally productive, giving always some increase, more or less according to the state of the times.

Well, then, this daily increase of "Demand Deposits" from the "Teller" windows is tossed into the safe, along with those "Time Deposits" from the window marked "Savings." Thus the bank accumulates deposits—that is to say, money. What does it do with the money? A bank pays interest; therefore, a bank must earn interest. It must earn more interest than it pays out, else it cannot make a profit for itself. So the bank must lend its deposits. To receive money on which it pays interest and to lend money on which it receives interest—that is a bank's whole business.

Now, what proportion of its total deposits do you suppose a bank lends? How much would you think it was safe to lend? The half? Three quarters? All? The fact is—and even those who know it well and take it for granted are astonished in those moments when they stop to reflect on it—the fabulous fact is that a bank may lend ten times its deposits. That is to say, for each actual dollar of other people's money it has received and locked up in its safe, it may lend or sell ten dollars of credit money.

Not every bank does lend ten to one—ten dollars of credit to one of cash in the vault; but if you take the banking system entire it has the potential power to erect credit in that ratio to cash. Ten to one was the formula adopted by the United States Treasury and other Federal Government agencies in their campaign against hoarding. In official messages broadcast over the country people were exhorted to stop hoarding and bring their money back to the banks on the ground that each dollar of actual money in hiding represented a loss of ten in the credit resources of the country, and that each dollar of money brought back to the banks represented an increase of ten dollars in credit for the common benefit of trade, commerce and industry.

The beginning of all modern credit phenomena is in this act of multiplication, performed by the banker. How can a bank lend credit to the amount of ten times its cash deposits?

Perhaps the easiest way to explain it will be to tell the story of the old goldsmiths who received gold for safe keeping and issued receipts for it. These receipts, representing the gold, began to pass from hand to hand as money. Seeing this, and that people seldom touched the gold itself or wanted it back, so long as they thought it was safe, the goldsmiths began to issue paper redeemable in gold, without having the gold in hand to redeem it with. A very audacious idea. And yet it was sound, or at least it worked, and if a goldsmith was honest he was solvent because in exchange for that paper, which he promised to redeem in gold on demand, he took things of value, called collateral, in pledge, so that against his outstanding paper he had good assets in hand, and if people did come with his paper, wanting the gold on it, he had only to sell those assets, buy the gold, then redeem the paper according to his promise—always provided the assets were liquid and easily sold and that too many people never came at once, all demanding gold on the instant. Fewer and fewer people ever did want the actual gold. So long as they believed in the goldsmith they preferred to use his paper for all purposes of exchange—paper which no longer represented the actual gold and yet was as good as gold and was counted as gold because whenever anybody did want the gold it was forthcoming. From this evolved modern banking. That circulating paper itself became legal money against which the banks were obliged by law and custom to keep a certain amount of gold in hand, called the gold reserve. The next step was to discover that upon this structure of legal paper money with a gold reserve behind it you could impose another strata of paper—a new free kind, redeemable either in gold or legal paper money. That new free kind of paper was the bank check we all know; and the use of bank checks in place of actual money has increased by habit and necessity until now we transact more than nine tenths of all our business by check, no actual money passing at all, or almost none. In the year 1929, for example, the total amount of actual money of all kinds in the country was nine billions; but the total exchange of bank checks was 713 billions, or nearly eighty times all the actual money in existence.

What a bank now lends is credit in the form of a blank check book. You use the credit by writing checks against it. You may write a check for cash and draw out actual money in the form of gold or legal paper money, but if you do and spend the money it will go straight back to the bank. When you borrow at the bank, what happens? The banker does not hand you the money. He writes down in the bank's own book a certain credit to your account and gives you a book of blank checks. Then you go out and begin to write checks against that credit. The people to whom you give the checks deposit them in the bank. As they deposit your checks the sums are charged to your account, deducted from your credit on the books. No actual money is involved.

If these last few passages have been difficult, take the fact lightly and without blame. Of all the discoveries and inventions by which we live and die this totally improbable helix of credit is the most cunning, the most liable, the least comprehended and, next to high explosives, the most dangerous. All that bankers themselves really know about it is how it works from day to day. Beyond that it is a gift from Pandora.

But you are still sitting in the local bank. Take it, if necessary, as an arbitrary fact that for each dollar of actual money that passes inward through those windows and stops in the safe the bank will have six, eight, maybe ten dollars of credit to lend. To whom does it lend this credit? And how?

There is a window yet to be observed, the one marked "Discounts and Collections." The transactions at this window take more time. Papers are signed and exchanged. These people are borrowers; they are attending to their loans, paying them off, or paying something on account, or arranging to have their promissory notes extended. One is the local contractor who has had to have credit on his note to pay for materials and labor while building a house;

the house is finished, he has been paid by the owner, and now he returns the credit by paying off his note—with a check. Another is the local automobile dealer who has just received from Detroit a carload of automobiles with draft attached, and the draft reads, "Pay at once." To pay the draft he must borrow credit at the bank; as he sells the automobiles one by one in the community he will return the credit—by check. Another is the radio dealer who sells radios on the instalment plan. He is borrowing credit against which he will write a check to pay the radio manufacturer for ten sets; as security for the loan he gives his own promissory note, together with the ten purchase contracts of the ten local people to whom he has sold the radio sets. As they pay him he will pay the bank—by check. Another is a farmer who has sold his crop and now is paying back—by check—the credit he borrowed six months ago to buy fertilizer and some new farm machinery.

Lending of this character, to local people, the bank knowing all of them personally, is not only the safest kind of lending for the bank; it is the ideal use of credit. Unfortunately, the local demand for credit is not enough to absorb the bank's whole lending power. From the savings of the community, always accumulating in the safe as cash deposits, the bank acquires a surplus lending power. Having satisfied its own customers with credit at the window marked "Discounts and Collections", what will the bank do with the surplus credit? Well, now you will see how credit, so rising at the obscure local source, overflows the source and begins to seek outlets to the lakes and gulfs and seas beyond—how its adventures begin.

The first thing the bank thinks to do with a part of its surplus credit is to lend it to a big New York City bank.

What will the New York bank do with it? The New York bank may lend it to a merchant in domestic trade or to one in the foreign trade; it may lend it to a broker on the Stock Exchange who lends it to a speculator; it may lend it in Europe to the Bank of England or it may lend it to a German bank where the interest rate is very high. Fancy local American credit, originating as you have seen, finding its way from this naïve source to a Berlin bank! Well, several hundreds of millions of just that kind of American credit did find its way to the banks of Germany and got trapped there in 1931. The German banks said they could not pay it back. That was what the moratorium was all about. Germany said if we insisted on having our credit back, her banks would simply shut up; she advised us to "freeze" it and leave it there on deposit in the German banks, in the hope that they might be able later to pay, and since there was nothing else to do we did that.

What else will the local bank do with its surplus credit? It will buy a United States government bond; it is simply lending this local credit to the Federal Government.

What will the Federal Government do with it? The Federal Government may give it to the Federal

Farm Board to support those wheat and cotton pyramids; the Federal Government may give it to the Reconstruction Finance Corporation, which will lend it to the railroads; the Federal Government may give it to the Veterans' Bureau, which will lend it to war veterans, or the Federal Government may spend it either to finish the memorial bridge across the Potomac River at Washington or for paper and lead pencils to be distributed on the desks of the Senate and House.

But the local bank has still a surplus of credit to lend. So far, by all the rules, it has been very conservative. The credit it has loaned to the big New York City bank is returnable on call. No worry about that. To get back the credit it has loaned to the United States Government it has only to sell the bond, and there is always an instant market for government bonds. So now the bank thinks it may take some risk, for the sake of obtaining a higher rate of interest.

You may notice a man talking very earnestly to the president at the desk behind the railing, and from something you read in his gestures you may take him to be a salesman. That is what he is—a bond salesman from Wall Street, and his merchandise this time is foreign bonds. He has some South American government bonds that pay seven per cent. and some German municipal bonds that pay eight per cent., and these are very attractive rates of interest, seeing that the bank pays its depositors only three and one half.

"You may think," the salesman is saying to the president, "that such rates of interest as seven and eight per cent. imply some risk in these bonds. Really there is no risk. The bonds are absolutely good. Foreign borrowers have to pay high rates of interest in this country, not because they are anything but good and solvent borrowers, but because our people are strange to foreign investments. That being temporarily so, this is a rare opportunity for a little bank like yours to make some very profitable investments."

So persuaded, the local bank with the remainder of its surplus credit buys foreign bonds. When it buys the bond of a South American Government, it is lending credit to that government, knowing no more about it than the salesman says. What will the South American Government do with that credit? Anything it likes, because it is a sovereign government; it may use it to build a gilded dome. Many new gilt domes have been built in foreign countries with just this kind of local American credit.

In buying the German bonds the bank is lending credit to the Free City of Bremen, perhaps, or to Cologne. What does the Free City of Bremen do with it? She may use it to widen the fairway of her harbor and build some new piers. The same credit might have been used to make ship channels and piers in the Hackensack Meadows of New Jersey. And what does Cologne do with it? She may use it to build a stadium or a great bathing pavilion for the happiness and comfort of her people. How strange! The local American community out of which this credit rises to perform such works in Germany has neither stadium nor swimming pool of its own. Or Cologne may use it to help build the largest new bridge in Europe across the Rhine, a bridge she really does not need, except to provide employment for her people. The same credit might be used to build a bridge across the Golden Gate at San Francisco.

One last observation before you leave the bank. How remote these people are from what is doing with the credit that rises from the dollars they leave at the windows! How little they know about it! Fancy telling that woman at the "Savings" window, who gets her money up in small bills from the deeps of an old satchel, that her dollars, multiplied ten times by the bank, will go to build ornaments for a grand boulevard in a little Latin-American country she never heard of, or to build workmen's houses in a German city better than the house she lives in. Fancy telling the man in overalls who comes next that his money, multiplied ten times by the bank, will go to a speculator on the New York Stock Exchange, or to mend a cathedral in Bavaria, or to a foreign bank that may lose it unless the matter of reparations is somehow settled in Europe, or that it may be loaned to Germany in order that Germany may pay reparations to the Allies in order that they may be willing to pay something on account of what they owe to the United States Treasury.

Remember as you leave the bank that it was one of 25,000, big and little, all performing the same act of multiplication, all in the same general ways lending the product of multiplication, which is credit. You have seen only one spring in the woods. Think of 25,000 such springs in the land, all continually overflowing with credit, and how this surplus local credit, seeking interest, by a law as unerring as the force of gravity finds its way to the streams that lead away to the lakes, gulfs and seas beyond. If you will keep this picture in suspense, you will better understand what else happens, if and when it does—and it is bound to happen from a reckless or deluded use of the power of credit.

There is a change in the economic heavens. Some stars fall out. On the ground some pyramids collapse. For two or three weeks what the Wall Street reporters call a debacle on the Stock Exchange holds first-page news position. Then one day a New York City bank with 400,000 depositors must paste a piece of paper in its plate-glass window, saying: "Closed by order of the State Bank Examiner." Of the surplus credit rising from the cash deposits of its forgotten 400,000 that bank has loaned too much on things such as afterward turn out to be pyramids—for example, skyscrapers.

Do you remember the old lady with the satchel at the window marked "Savings" in the small local bank? She has a friend in New York City who was one of the 400,000. She gets a letter from this friend, saying a bank these days is no place for one's money.

It will be safer, even though without interest, in many places a woman can think of. It may be the bottom of the flour can. So this old lady appears again at the window marked "Savings." She wants all her money out. Then the man in overalls comes; he has heard something to the same effect and he wants all of his money out. These two would not matter to the great American banking system as a whole. But remember, this is one of 25,000 banks, in each one of which a few depositors are asking for their money back, all at one time. This, then, is the beginning of that contraction in all the springs and streams and waters of credit that was spoken of before.

What now takes place is the reverse of multiplication. It is deflation. The banker cannot control it. If he has multiplied credit in the ratio of ten for one, so, as his depositors take away their money, he must reduce credit in the same ratio. That is to say, for each dollar of cash that is taken out of his hands, he must call back from somewhere ten dollars of credit. Thus the vast and sensitive mechanism of credit, running at high speed, is put suddenly in reverse motion, with a frightful clashing of gears.

Return to the case of the little local bank, where you were sitting. As its depositors continue to withdraw cash, it must call in credit. First it sends word by telephone or telegraph to the big New York City bank, saying: "Please return our credit. We need it."

But since the New York bank, remember, has loaned that credit out, it must in turn call it back from some one else. If it has loaned it on the Stock

Exchange to brokers, who have loaned it to speculators, these must give it back. But suppose the New York City banks that supply the Stock Exchange with credit are all calling at the same time for it to be returned, because thousands of local banks all over the country, where the credit came from, are calling upon them to return it.

In that case the Stock Exchange brokers are sunk. They cannot replace the credit they are called upon to give up, because the sources of credit are now contracting. This being the fact, the brokers say to their customers, namely, the speculators: "We are sorry and this is awful, but there is no more credit. The banks are calling our loans. We cannot carry your securities any longer on credit. If you cannot pay for them in cash in the next fifteen minutes, we shall have to sell them for what they will bring, to save ourselves."

From this cause there is a new day of panic on the Stock Exchange, a further debacle, with hideous wide headlines in the papers. Panic is advertised. The whirling Stock Exchange pyramid is falling, for want of credit to sustain it. This is an effect that becomes in turn a cause. Because of the headlong decline in prices on the Stock Exchange, in which the loss of imaginary wealth is measured, and for other reasons not exactly given, more banks fail. Each day the lines of anxious depositors grow longer. Thus the waters of credit continue to contract, and the rate is accelerated.

But suppose the New York bank has loaned the credit to a bank in Berlin and cannot get it back at all.

What will it do in that case? For it is obliged either to return the credit to the small local bank that is demanding it back or confess itself insolvent. Well, in that case the New York bank must sell some securities out of its own reserve investments. But if all the New York banks are doing the same thing at the same time, as more or less they will be, the effect on the Stock Exchange is even worse. The banks will be selling bonds where speculators would be selling only stocks, and the effect upon the mind of the country from a fall in bonds is much more disturbing.

Now what you are looking at is liquidation. Credit is contracting because these thousands of forgotten bank depositors are calling for their money; and because credit is contracting everybody is calling at once for the return of it to its source, and there is no way for the person who last borrowed to return it but to sell something.

Suppose, however, that the local bank gets its credit back from the New York bank. It is not enough. Its depositors continue to take their money out; more credit must be called in—always, remember, ten for one. Somebody, somewhere, must give up ten dollars of credit for each dollar of actual money the depositors withdraw. The local bank next thinks of selling its South American bonds. That is another way of calling credit back. Somebody will have to buy the bonds, of course, but that simply means that whoever buys them from the bank will be taking the bank's place as creditor of the South

American Government that issued the bonds. The bank need not worry about who that buyer is; the transaction will take place in the open bond market, where the law of *caveat emptor* holds. Buyer, beware. But when the local bank goes to sell its South American bonds it finds them quoted at thirty—the same bonds it paid ninety for. The South American Government is in financial trouble, and all the buyers standing in the bond market know it; that is why they will offer only thirty for the bonds. If the bank sells them at thirty it will have lost forever two thirds of the credit it loaned to the South American Government. Besides, if that is all it can get for the bonds, it will not greatly help to sell them. So it puts these bonds aside and looks at its German bonds. But German bonds also have collapsed. Their condition may be as bad, or worse, because Germany is in trouble. What else can the bank sell? It can sell its United States government bonds; yet even in these there is a considerable loss. They have declined in price under the selling of hundreds, thousands, of other banks all in the same dilemma, all tempted to sell their United States government bonds instead of worse bonds on which they cannot afford to take the loss.

Having got back the credit it loaned to the United States Government, by selling its United States government bonds, the local bank goes on for a while, paying off its depositors, exhorting them to desist, telling them everything will be all right, hoping for the best. Then one day the Bank Examiner from the

Comptroller's office at Washington comes unexpectedly to look at the books and decide if the bank is solvent. Having looked at the books he says: "See here! You have sold all of your best assets. Now to make your books balance with bad assets you still value them at what you paid for them. These foreign bonds, for example—still valued on your books at ninety and ninety-five when you know very well they are worth in the market to-day only thirty or thirty-five. You are not a solvent bank. You will have to close."

Then the fatal piece of white paper is pasted on the plate glass, and all the depositors then at the windows asking for their money are put out.

That—almost exactly that—happened to 3,635 banks of all kinds in the two years 1930 and 1931. The deposits of these 3,635 ruined banks were more than 2½ billions of dollars.

It is easily forgotten that the depositor who stands outside to read the Bank Examiner's verdict through the glass was the original lender.

Consider what it is a depositor does. It is clear enough that when he makes a deposit he is lending money to the bank. But what does the money represent? If it is earned money the depositor brings, it represents something of equal value produced by his own exertions, something he would sooner save than consume. It may be a cord of wood. Suppose it.

There are only a few things to do with a surplus cord of wood. If you store it for your own future use it represents earned leisure. If you exchange it with a neighbor for something else you want that is conversion by crude barter. In neither case is there any increase. It is all the time one cord of wood. You may sell it for money. If you hoard the money you have the equivalent of one cord of wood and yet no increase. But suppose you take the money to the bank and leave it there at interest. In that case you have loaned the bank your surplus labor to the value of a cord of wood, and there is the beginning of increase. Another industrious man, who is without tools, borrows money from the bank to buy an ax, a maul and some wedges. These tools represent your cord of wood. With these tools that man chops three cords of wood. One he wants for himself and two he sells. With the proceeds of one he returns to the bank the money he borrowed to buy the tools. He has still in his hand the proceeds of the third cord, which is profit or increase. Let him resolve, instead of spending the increase, to save it. He puts it in the bank. Now the bank has two cords of wood where there was but one before—not the cordwood itself, not the labor itself, but the money agent of labor; besides which are the tools still in the man's hand. All this from one surplus cord of wood to begin with.

Thus we accumulate wealth, and there is no limit to it, provided the labor is not lost.

Now suppose a third man comes and borrows all of that money to build a toy in the meaning of a pyramid that has no economic value, or to make an unlucky speculation, or to buy something he is impatient to enjoy before he has produced anything of equivalent value and then afterward fails to produce the equivalent, so that it turns out that he is unable to pay interest or return the principal. We say in that case the money is lost. Really it is not. It still exists. But what the money represented is lost, and that was the amount of labor necessary to produce two cords of wood.

There is neither value nor power in money itself, only in what it represents. Every dollar of actual money should betoken that a dollar's worth of wealth has been somewhere in some form produced; every dollar of credit multiplied upon that money by the banker should signify that somewhere in some form a dollar's worth of wealth is in process of creation.

Anything that happens to money to debase it, to degrade its relation to the total sum of wealth, so as to impair its buying power, is something that happens to people who have loaned their labor to the banks.

Why do we confine the function of money issue to the government, and have very rigid laws concerning the exercise of that function by the government, and make counterfeiting a crime? All that is with the idea of keeping the value of money constant, for if money is permitted to increase faster than the wealth of things which we price in money, then the value of labor saved in the form of money will deteriorate like a cord of wood in the weather. When for any reason a government is moved to embrace legal counterfeiting, when it begins to issue spurious money—money that has no definite relation to any form of wealth in being or in process—the sequel is well known. There is progressive inflation, which, once it begins, there is no stopping or controlling, short of the final disaster. At the end, the savings of a lifetime, reconverted into money, may not be enough to buy a hat.

This we have learned about money itself, dimly. We have yet to learn it about credit, even dimly.

To any suggestion that the government shall set its printing presses free and flood the country with fiat money, all our economic intelligence reacts with no. Only those will say yes who are mentally or politically unsound. And if a government is obliged by vote of the unsound to do it, then everybody, including the unsound, will begin to hoard gold because gold is the one kind of money no government can make or dilute. Or if it were proposed that every bank should have the privilege to issue money as it might think fit, entirely in its own discretion, we should all know better. Even banks would say no to that. It is not only that people cannot trust private bankers with that privilege; private bankers would be unwilling to trust one another with it.

Yet on this jealously guarded base of money itself, banks are free to inflate and multiply credit, each in its own discretion, notwithstanding the fact that the inflation of money and the inflation of credit are similar evils, producing similar miseries. Inflation of credit—ecstasy, delusion, fantastic enrichment. Deflation of credit—depression, crisis, remorse. One state succeeds the other and there is no escape, for one is cause and one is effect.

Printed in the United States
By Bookmasters